PORTUGAL

Prec
was
defe
cent
of P
long
pag
boa
in t
Tov
com
at t
Dis

DISTRI *Cultural*

A qualidade da literatura

GRUPO
DISTRI

But the Portuguese faced serious competition for the trading posts they had established overseas. Other European nations—especially Spain—rushed to follow their lead, and for a small country, with a population to match, maintaining a strong presence around the globe proved an increasing strain. As a result, an exhausted Portugal fell under Spanish control for a 60-year period beginning in 1580. During this time, the Spanish neglected the Portuguese trading centers and other nations moved in, causing Portugal to lose many of its trading monopolies in the East and in Africa.

After Portuguese nobles won the country's independence back from Spain in 1640, Portugal experienced a second boom created by colonial trade. This time it was the gold and diamonds of Brazil, which Portugal had discovered in 1500. Once again, the aristocracy felt rich, and João V, who took the throne in 1706, and the aristocrats of his court, brought in foreign architects to create magnificent baroque structures. This bountiful period only lasted through the mid-eighteenth century. When João's son, José I, ascended to the throne, he gave almost complete power to his prime minister, the Marquês do Pombal, who, despite his oppressive, dictatorial rule, in many

Ancient walls with square towers still encircle Óbidos near the Estremaduran coast, a town of such charm that Portugal's kings ceremoniously presented it to their new queens for more than 600 years. *Below:* Sunlight breaks dramatically through storm clouds onto the rugged cliffs and fishing village of Nazaré.

Traditional energy sources like this windmill towering over a residential street in Peniche are still actively used in Portugal. *Below:* The women of Peniche work together to mend the nets of the town's fishing fleet.

Near Lindoso, eighteenth- and nineteenth-century *espiguleros,* or granaries, are still used for drying corn. *Below:* An ornate stairway lined with statues winds 381 feet uphill to Bom Jesus Church, a frequent destination of devoted pilgrims, on the outskirts of Braga. *Opposite:* In Monsanto, houses share the mountainside with the granite boulders from which they were built. The town was designed in ancient times to blend into the rocky slopes.

The brilliant hues of this fleet of fishing boats gleam in the subtropical Madeiran sun. *Above:* Azulejos soften the austere lines of a Madeiran church.

Index of Pl

All photograph

Page Numbe

IRAQ
the culture

April Fast

A Bobbie Kalman Book
The Lands, Peoples, and Cultures Series

Crabtree Publishing Company
www.crabtreebooks.com

Palaces

The kings and leaders of Mesopotamia and modern Iraq have always built magnificent palaces in which to live. Isa ibn Musa, a wealthy prince, built Ukhaydir Palace in the desert southwest of Karbala in the late 700s. The **fortified** complex included a mosque, palace, and bathhouse, or separate building for bathing.

In 1982, Saddam Hussein rebuilt the Babylon palace of King Nebuchadnezzar II, who ruled from 605 to 562 B.C. Archaeologists disagreed with the project because they believed it would ruin the ancient site. Hussein also built a new palace for himself in Babylon, with high ceilings, spiral staircases, arched entryways, endless marble, and exquisite furniture. Since the overthrow of his government, thieves have stripped the palace of many of its treasures.

Modern architecture

The best examples of modern architecture in Iraq are in Baghdad. The designs of many of the city's art galleries, museums, hotels, and public libraries are inspired by Muslim architecture. Muslim architecture is famous for its use of domes and gilding, along with colorful tile **mosaics**, pillars, arches, and stonework.

(above) Saddam Hussein built 55 lavish palaces during his rule, which lasted from 1979 to 2003. The presidential complex in Tikrit, in northern Iraq, is composed of several palaces built next to the Tigris River. The site was destroyed in April 2003 by U.S. warplanes.

(below) In the 1700s and 1800s, some homes in Baghdad, Mosul, and Basra had screened balconies called shanashils. The screens were often made of wood carved into delicate patterns. Many of these homes still stand today.

The ancient Mesopotamians were great creators and inventors. The Sumerians, who ruled from about 3500 B.C. to 2300 B.C., are believed to have invented the wheel and the twelve-month calendar. Each month began when the first sliver of a new moon appeared.

Cuneiform

Writing was one of Mesopotamia's greatest accomplishments. It was developed by the Sumerians around 3200 B.C. The first writing consisted of pictures that **scribes** etched into wet clay with a pointed instrument called a stylus. The stylus was made from the stems of reeds or pieces of bone or wood. Soon, a wedge-shaped tip replaced the point, and straight lines were drawn instead of complete pictures to save time. This system of lines came to be known as cuneiform, for the **Latin** words *cuneus*, meaning "wedge," and *forma*, meaning "shape."

(top) The earliest cuneiform writings were simple lists or records of traded items, such as animals, grains, or vegetables. Numbers were expressed by repeating lines or circles. This carved tablet is a record of horses and sheep to be sacrificed.

Laws

The Sumerian king Ur-Nammu established some of the first laws in the world around 2050 B.C. Known as the Code of Ur-Nammu, they dealt with topics such as marriage, divorce, theft, injury to others, and owning land. The Babylonian king Hammurabi, who ruled from 1792 to 1750 B.C., wrote his own set of 282 laws, known as the Code of Hammurabi. They were carved on tablets and displayed throughout his empire.

The following are some examples of his laws:
- Law 25: If a fire breaks out in a house and the person who comes to put it out steals the owner's property, the thief shall be thrown into the fire.
- Law 55: If a person opens his ditches to water his crops and the water floods his neighbor's field, he shall pay his neighbor corn for the loss.

(below) This stele, or stone pillar, contains a section of the Code of Hammurabi. At the top of the stele is the sun god, Shamash, dictating his laws to Hammurabi.

Babylonians used different stones for weighing different items. Many of the stones were finely shaped and polished, such as this weight in the shape of a goose.

Weights and measures

Ancient Mesopotamians developed standard, or widely accepted, ways to weigh and measure goods. This helped keep business fair and easy to understand for traders from different lands. At first, standard weights were based on real items. For example, a "donkey load" was based on how much weight a donkey could carry. Then, the Babylonians developed a system of weighing items against standard-sized stones.

The first known standard tool for measurement was a copper bar called the Cubit of Nippur, developed in 1950 B.C. The bar was about 20 inches (51 centimeters) long and divided into equal portions, like a ruler. The Sumerians also established the length of a foot in 2575 B.C., likely to measure cloth. It remains the oldest standard of length in the world today.

Cylinder seals

Cylinder seals were like miniature rolling pins that were usually made of stone. They were carved with images of gods, religious ceremonies, animals, and plants, as well as hunting scenes. Mesopotamians used the seals from about 3000 B.C. to the end of the 400s A.D. to sign documents written on clay tablets and to mark property. Seals were sometimes rolled onto mud bricks before they hardened to indicate when buildings were constructed and who constructed them. People also wore seals as jewelry, since they were believed to protect against illness and danger.

Sometimes, the figures on cylinder seals were arranged in decorative patterns, but more often they showed an action.

The majority of Iraqis speak Arabic, the language of the *Qur'an*, but many other languages are heard in the country's markets and streets. English is the most common western language in Iraq, and is often used along with Arabic as a language of instruction in universities.

Arabic

Arabs conquered Mesopotamia in the 600s A.D., but their language arrived two centuries earlier, as Arabic-speaking tribes began moving into the area. Today, Arabic is the official language of most parts of Iraq. It has 29 letters, 26 consonants, and 3 vowels, and is written from right to left. The languages of neighboring countries have influenced the form of Arabic spoken in Iraq, such as as Persian and Turkish words that became part of the Iraqi vocabulary.

Kurdish

Iraq's Kurds live mainly in a northern part of the country known as the Kurdish Autonomous Region, or Iraqi Kurdistan. The region was set aside in 1974 for Kurds to rule independently.

The official language of the area, Kurdish, is related to ancient Persian languages. There are two main **dialects**, Kurdi, or Sorani, and Kermanji. Kurdi is spoken in the south of Iraqi Kurdistan, and is the official form of Kurdish in the region. Kermanji is spoken by Kurds in the north of the region. Both dialects are written in Arabic script in Iraq, and most Kurds can understand both.

(above) Kurdish street vendors have a lively discussion in the shopping district of Irbil, a city in the north.

(top) Students test each other before an exam at the University of Baghdad. In times of peace, many languages can be heard at the university, where students from Iraq, as well as other Arab and foreign countries, study.

English	Arabic	Kurdi
Hello.	*Marhaba.*	*Bakher been.*
Goodbye.	*Maa' elSalama.*	*Khwa hafiz.*
How are you?	*Kaif halak?*	*Jone?*
I am fine.	*Ana bikhair.*	*Bashim.*
What sports do you play?	*Ay riyada tala'b?*	*Jewavza shek akai?*
My favorite sport is soccer.	*Ma riyadatak el Mofadala*	*Tob tobeen.*

Turkmen

Turkmen began moving into Iraq in the 600s and now live in the north and northeast, especially near the city of Kirkuk. They speak Turkmen, a Turkic language. Most Iraqi Turkmen write their language using the Arabic script, even though a Roman-based alphabet of 28 letters was introduced for writing the language in the 1990s. No schools in Iraq currently teach in Turkmen, but the Turkmen people, as well as other Iraqi peoples, are working with the government to gain the right to be educated in both Arabic and their native languages.

This Turkmen boy serves bread at a restaurant in the northern city of Kirkuk. Kirkuk is home to Turkmen, Kurds, and Arabs. The languages of all three ethnic groups can be heard on the city's streets.

Aramaic

Aramaic was the common language of ancient Mesopotamia from about 700 B.C. to 700 A.D. Today, there are several dialects of Aramaic, each with its own script. Nestorian and Chaldean Assyrians speak an eastern dialect of Aramaic called Syriac. Other eastern dialects of Aramaic include Mandaic, which is spoken by a small population of Iraqi Mandaeans. All dialects of Aramaic are written from right to left and do not have number symbols. Instead, combinations of letters represent numbers.

Persian

The Persian language, also known as Farsi, can be traced back to the 500s B.C. It is the language of Iran, which was formerly known as Persia. It is spoken by the Persian population in Iraq, who live around Iraq's holy cities. Not only has Persian influenced the Arabic language spoken in Iraq, but more than 40 percent of modern Persian words are borrowed from Arabic. Persian is written using the Arabic script.

Storytelling and poetry

The earliest Mesopotamian writings were prayers to the gods, heroic tales, stories of battles, and **myths**. Many of these were set to music and sung at weddings, after battles, or at funerals. Storytelling was a popular pastime in Mesopotamia, and is still popular in Iraq today.

The Thousand and One Nights

The Thousand and One Nights is a collection of popular stories woven into one larger tale. The storyteller Al-Jahshiyari was most likely the first to write it down in Iraq in the 900s. *The Thousand and One Nights* tells of a woman named Scheherazade who marries the king Sharyar. Sharyar was known for marrying a new wife every day, only to have her killed the next morning. To save herself, Scheherazade told her husband a story on the very first night of their marriage, and promised to continue the next evening. The king was so enchanted by Scheherazade's stories that he allowed her to live.

Many editions of The Thousand and One Nights *have been published over the years. This illustration is from an 1895 edition.*

An ancient library

King Ashurbanipal oversaw one of the first libraries in the world, in the ancient city of Nineveh. The Assyrian king, who ruled from 668 to 627 B.C., collected Mesopotamian poems and stories, historical accounts, business contracts, government documents, and scientific texts. Archaeologists uncovered his library, complete with 25,000 clay tablets, between 1849 and 1851. These writings give a glimpse into what life was like for Sumerian, Akkadian, and Assyrian civilizations.

Modern poetry

Poetry has long been Iraq's traditional form of writing. Iraqi poems have explored love, politics, and social problems. In the 1970s, the government began to take control of the literature produced in the country. Poets and other writers were not allowed to make negative comments about the ruling Ba'th Party. Many left the country, and those who stayed were encouraged to praise their leader, Saddam Hussein, in their works. One of Iraq's best-known modern poets is Saadi Youssef, whose collections include *Without an Alphabet, Without a Face*. He left Iraq in 1979 and now lives in London, England.

Saadi Youssef's poetry has been translated into many languages. Youssef is also a respected translator of English literature into Arabic.

Bedouin poetry

The Bedouin considered their poets to be important keepers of history, honoring events and people in long, detailed stories told in verse. Poets often sang or chanted to others around the evening fire, and those listening would memorize the poems. In the 700s, a man named Hammad al-Rawiha wrote down all the Bedouin poetry he had memorized. This famous collection of verse is known as the *Mu'allaqat*.

Kurdish literature

Kurdish Iraqis are known for their fantasy stories, as well as for their chanted poems about war and love. The Kurdish poet Ahmed Khani wrote the epic *Mem-o-zin* in 1695. This love story gives a detailed look into Kurdish history and the Kurds' hopes of becoming a nation.

The Kurds, as well as Iraqi Arabs, also have a strong tradition of proverbs. The saying "What matters is the menu on the table now" stresses the importance of living in the present. "The only friends we have are the mountains" reflects the Kurdish people's history of isolation and mistreatment. Modern Kurdish literature focuses on Kurdish issues, as well, such as struggles with the Iraqi government.

The Iraqi novel

Modern Iraqi novels tend to tell of life under government control, struggles between groups and individuals, and the general concerns of Arabs. Yousif al-Haydari's *Man and Cockroach*, published in 1964, tells the story of a man who is afraid of society. The novel expresses a feeling of powerlessness against the political situation of the time. Muhsin al-Ramli's book *Scattered Crumb*, published in 2003, tells of a peasant family falling apart as a father and son clash over Saddam Hussein's rule.

Iraqi author Nawal Nasrallah, who now lives in Boston, holds a copy of her cookbook Delights from the Garden of Eden: A Cookbook and a History of the Iraqi Cuisine. *Nasrallah wrote the book in the hope that it would keep Iraqi cooking alive for the many Iraqis who fled their country for the United States and other English-speaking countries.*

The Epic of Gilgamesh

The Epic of Gilgamesh was discovered on twelve clay tablets in King Ashurbanipal's library at Nineveh. Written in the ancient Akkadian language, it tells of the adventures of Gilgamesh, the legendary king of the city of Uruk, who lived around 2700 B.C. After his friend Enkidu died, Gilgamesh set out to discover the secret of immortality, or everlasting life.

Gilgamesh and Utnapishtim

Gilgamesh traveled to a dark, cold land called the Far-Away to find Utnapishtim, a man who had survived a great flood in Babylon and been granted immortality. Gilgamesh hoped that Utnapishtim would share the secret of everlasting life with him.

Many rivers joined at the Far-Away before running into the ocean. By the banks of those rivers stood Utnapishtim. Gilgamesh pleaded with him, "Please, you must tell me how I can live forever, like you."

Utnapishtim sighed and looked across the rivers. "Gilgamesh, nothing is meant to live forever. Human beings are meant to live their lives, do their best, and pass on so another generation can do the same. Just like these rivers run their course and eventually end in the ocean, so too life comes to an end. Everlasting life can be lonely and terrible," he added.

Gilgamesh grew upset. "I want to live forever. You must tell me how to become immortal," he insisted.

Utnapishtim nodded his head slowly. "As you wish," he whispered. "There is a plant at the bottom of the ocean that surrounds the Far-Away. You must swim to the bottom of the ocean and snatch the plant. Eat the magic plant, and you will be young again."

Gilgamesh thanked Utnapishtim and immediately went to the water's edge. He dove into the ocean and swam with all his might to the very bottom, where he found the magic plant. Filled with joy, he rose up from the water and climbed back onto land. "I have the plant!" he announced. "Now, I shall never die."

He held the plant firmly in his hand, said goodbye to Utnapishtim, and summoned the **ferryman** to take him home. As they crossed the River of Death, Gilgamesh fell asleep. When he awoke, he wailed in despair, for in his hand he held nothing.

"Oh, gods of the heavens!" he cried. "I have lost the magic plant!"

He looked into the river just in time to see a snake disappearing into the dark water with the magic plant in his mouth. "You, serpent! You have stolen from me! Now you shall be forever young, and I shall die!"

Saddened by his loss, Gilgamesh arrived at the gates of his city, where he beheld his wonderful kingdom. The sight of all that he had built made Gilgamesh happier.

"If I cannot live forever, I must at least find a way to make a difference in the world. I will build a strong empire filled with wonderful structures. I will show the people how to be kind to one another. I will live the best way I can, so that in the end, my life will have meaning." With that, Gilgamesh approached his city with outstretched arms and peace in his heart.

 # Glossary

apprentice A person learning a skill by working with someone who is more experienced

archaeologist A person who studies the past by looking at buildings and artifacts

architecture The art of designing and constructing buildings

artisan A skilled craftsperson

baptize To sprinkle with water or dip in water as part of a Christian ceremony

censor To examine a book, film, or other publication in order to delete or change parts that are considered offensive

coalition A temporary political union for a particular purpose

dialect A version of a language spoken in one region

dowry The money or property that a bride brings to her groom when they marry

equinox Either of two times during the year when day and night are of equal length

ethnic Describing groups with the same nationality, customs, religion, or race

ferryman A person who transports people or goods in a boat

fertility The capacity to grow, as with plants, or have children

fortified Strengthened against attacks

glorify To make something seem more pleasant than it actually is

improvisation Something made up and performed without preparation

Latin The language of the ancient Romans

lyre An ancient string instrument resembling a harp

modesty The state of dressing and acting in a proper, respectable way

monarchy A government that is ruled by a king, queen, emperor, or empress

mosaic A design made from small pieces of stone, glass, or tile

mystical Spiritual

myth A traditional story about a god or another being with superhuman powers

nomadic Having no fixed home and moving from place to place in search of food and water

Ottoman A member of a Turkish dynasty

pagan Related to a belief in spirits in nature

pilgrimage A religious journey to a sacred place

prophet A person believed to deliver messages from God

reflection Careful thought

republic A country led by an elected government rather than a king or queen

ritual A religious ceremony in which steps must be followed in a certain order

rival Opposing

sacrifice The act of killing an animal in a religious ceremony as an offering to the gods

scribe A person who copies manuscripts and documents

shrine A holy place dedicated to a god or saint

temple A building used for religious services

underworld The imaginary place of the dead below the earth

Zoroastrian Related to a religion that was developed in ancient Iran by the prophet Zoroaster. It is based on the idea that there is a continuous fight between a god who represents good and one who represents evil

Index

1 2 3 4 5 6 7 8 9 0 Printed in the U.S.A. 3 2 1 0 9 8 7 6 5 4